Create Your Business Plan in 1-Week

A Step-by-Step Tool to Guide You in Creating an Effective Business Plan

Jonathan Croft

Table of Contents

A. Introduction

So, you are set and ready to start your own business. Your nerves are building in anticipation for what will be coming next and the world before you is full of potential. The potential for success combines with nerves for the hurdles that are unknown on the road that so many before have followed. In the United States, and throughout the world, hundreds of businesses start the road to success every day. The development of an effective and usable business plan is the first tool that can be utilized to help an entrepreneur give themselves the best opportunity for success. In the following book, we will uncover specific details and suggestions as how to best communicate with a targeted audience to achieve a desired outcome by application of a business plan.

B. How to Use This Book

Every craftsman needs a tool belt. This book is geared toward you as an Entrepreneur and will allow for a continual tool to look back on as your journey continues in developing a successful startup business. From your first business plan, to one down the road as your business transitions from startup to veteran, this book will allow you to view an Entrepreneur's perspective on how to create success. The book will help you to think and act like a multi-national corporation with vision and structure, but will enable you to enhance your competitive edge within localities and specific marketplaces that you focus upon. The book can be read from beginning to end, or you may utilize the Table of Contents to get directly to the advice that you need the most for a given situation that you may be facing.

Just as every startup business is unique, so too is the ability to vary the utilization of this book. Some aspects of your business or organization may directly correlate to a specific topic or recommended feature of a business plan, while others may simply not make sense to include in your personal business plan. This book is to be utilized as a guideline with additional resources and tips that will make your business plan attractive and effective, not only today, but into the future.

C. The Importance of Having the Right Mindset Before Starting a Business

Positivity. Positivity. Positivity.

Having the right mindset before, during, and after starting a business is more important than any business plan you will ever develop or read. Without the right mindset, quite simply, there is no plan. As an entrepreneur and business owner, you are your own worst critic, and at the same time, you are your own best supporter and advocate. The right mindset when starting a business means having the ability to think positive towards the future but also in a realistic frame of mind. This means that when advice is given by those around you, especially those that have had experience in a related field or industry, you should take it. It is critical to have an open mind for new ideas and feedback. Remember that you can always learn something new. Even Einstein, himself, continued to learn and develop theories day after day. Correlate this mindset of continual success and openness to learning in your path of starting a business.

Positivity, just as important, is in relation to the competition. Respect your competition and know that you can also learn from them to become a better, more advanced, small business and business leader in that relationship. In a world marketplace, competition is inevitable and must be embraced, respected, and give you the opportunity to remain positive in your own outlook in your small business adventure. Competition is what makes you better and is what helps make those goals that you will soon achieve so great to accomplish. Stay positive and positivity will follow.

Positivity through the best of times and the worst of times. As a business owner, you will face challenges and obstacles in your journey of developing a small business along with successes. It is important to stay positive and continually be open to learning through these obstacles and challenges, always with the goal of becoming better or more efficient in what you do and at a higher competitive level. Remember, that if the road was easy, everyone would travel on it. It takes the best to reach the destination, and you are already on the right road.

By selecting this book you have already made the key decision that success, not failure, is the term glorified in your vocabulary. You are ready to uphold a positive mindset and continue to learn. You are ready to start a business, which according to *Forbes*, has the ability to succeed as 28 Million small businesses alongside you have done previously. You have the mindset and are ready to embrace success and what it will take to get there.

D. Crafting Your Message

A business plan is a tool utilized by entrepreneurs to enable success in motion. A small business is fluid, always changing and developing in relation to surrounding variables. A business plan helps to create a game plan for triumph along the way, in which, allows an entrepreneur to embrace the fluidity of business and use variabilities to maintain a successful outcome. This is where crafting your message becomes important in developing a business plan. A business plan is an essential tool that creates structure for your business through a specific message that is both qualitative and quantitative. The message that you create in a business plan is also critical in relation to the target for which you are trying to reach, as we will discuss in the next section.

E. Identifying Your Target

There are two key targets that can be of focus when developing a business plan, and what is incorporated within those plans is varied based on the target that you choose as a business owner and entrepreneur. Crafting a message for you to look back upon for weeks, months, or years in business development will be vastly different than a message that is crafted with the goal to obtain investors for your small business venture. Throughout this book, we will look at valuable tools that can be incorporated with both goals in mind, but first, here is a summary of what the target differences are for a business plan.

Small Business Plan for Investors

A small business plan that has a message crafted for investors is going to be highly quantitative-based. Moreover, a business plan that is geared toward an Investor-target audience will be focused on the bottom line and what activities and processes will lead to the biggest bottom line possible. When investors are your identified target for a business plan, items such as Break-Even Analysis and Projected Cash Flows stream highly in the mindset of an investor as they are resources that help provide an outlook on what this business will mean to them. Just as this small business means the world to you, the same business will also mean a lot to those that are considered stakeholders and investors.

An investor of a small business venture wants to know what activities and plans you have in place to meet the goals that you are setting to achieve and they want to know that those activities will lead to a realistic outcome. Over-optimism is a big NO NO when it comes to communicating with an investor. Be realistic in your communication through a business plan and be realistic in what your business will achieve with their assistance, and in turn, be realistic in what they should expect to receive as a benefit from their investment. As a business owner looking to communicate with investors through a business plan, remember that when you succeed, they succeed, and success breeds success.

Small Business Plan for You

Ok, we have talked about the realistic goals and what it means to communicate those to a potential investor for your small business, but how about you as an entrepreneur? As an entrepreneur you are an investor as well. You are getting ready to, or have already started, a journey that will take countless hours, days, weeks, months and years. As a small business owner you do not have the opportunity to go home at night and turn off the thinking-cap; as a small business owner and entrepreneur, you are a constant investor, always looking for the best way to operate your business or looking for the next client that will help impact your bottom line.

So, how do you communicate to yourself through a business plan? Along the same lines as communicating with a potential investor, you want to have clear processes and actions identified and the goals that you are looking to obtain through those actions. Be honest with yourself in what it will take to get to where you want to be, but when developing a business plan for yourself, remember that this will be a tool for success for many years to come, not just today. So, with that in mind, do not be afraid to dream, and dream BIG. Take the time to incorporate the big dreams of where you want this business to go. Today, your basement office of 200 square feet, but tomorrow, your multi-national business with locations across the globe meets the needs of your diverse client-base.

Dream big, because it will be important to have the "Whys" available along the way. When the nights get long and the weekends seem to be non-existent, you need to be able to come back to this business plan and see the goals that you have set for the future and remember where you started and where you knew this could go, and will go.

F. Guide to a Business Plan

At this point, you should now know for whom you are writing a business plan and for what reasons you are writing. Remember to have a positive mindset as you take this journey, and remember that each step along the expedition allows you to become closer to the goals that you set, not only for yourself, but for your business, your family, and your community. In the sections following, we will go step-by-step in creating a business plan that will be a tool for continual success for your organization.

1. Cover Page

They say that you can't read a book by its cover. That phrase is not always true in the world of small business. Often times, a logo or brand is what identifies a sale. Take an example of walking with a child down a cereal aisle at your local grocery store. What is at eye-level for a child through every cereal aisle in every grocery chain throughout the country? It definitely isn't wheat-bran or fiber and berries; no, brands jumping out with bright colors and animated characters grab the focus of the targeted audience reaching for, often, sugar-packed and flavor enriched cereals. Parents are not the ones judging by the cover, but the target audience of the child reaching over the grocery cart for their favorite brand of cereal is doing just that, judging by the cover. The cereal that is inside is none to be judged, but the image and brand on the outside makes the sale.

Take this example to heart when developing a cover page of a business plan. The cover page sets the initial tone for what is to be seen throughout the remainder of the plan within. Is your small business exciting or boring? Is your small business worth investing in? The amount of time and effort that you place into a cover page may need to be more of an allocation than you had originally thought. If you have not done so already, ensure that you have a business logo that is in alignment with what your business is aiming to achieve. If you have not already thought of what your business logo will be, utilize the resources and individuals around you to develop one.

Here are some helpful ideas to consider in where to get assistance in developing a logo that will stand out and that will also not break the bank:

- Graphic Arts Student at your local Community College
- Tattoo Artist
- Online database with available logo options
- Have your own child, niece or nephew, come up with a doodle or scribble after you tell them your business name- it might just be the next "Nike Swoosh"

After identifying what logo you will incorporate on your cover page, as well as throughout all marketing material and documents to be produced by your business from this point forward, you need to identify the primary overview of your business. In addition to having a welcoming and unique format to the cover letter, there are some key pieces of information that must always be included:

- Business Name
- Business Owner (You) and additional Key Individuals to the Business
- Basic Contact Information

- Goal of the Business Plan/Mission statement of the Business Plan (Note that this is not the mission statement for your business, itself, but the mission for what you hope that the business plan will achieve for your business)

It is sometimes easy to get caught up in the intricacies of a cover page and it can quickly turn from clean and direct to cluttered and sloppy. Avoid cluttered and sloppy. Keep it simple, but professional. If you are trying to fit something else into the cover page, take it out, there is room for it elsewhere in the business plan. This is your cereal box; make sure that your audience wants to grab it off the shelf from first glance before anyone else can get a hold of it.

2. Executive Summary

Even though the Executive Summary is the first portion of the business plan to be analyzed, it should be the last item to be written when developing the plan. An Executive Summary helps to summarize the most important points that will be portrayed in the following business plan, including objectives and the vision that business is working to achieve into the future. The Executive Summary provides the opportunity to establish an initial timeline for goal achievement as well as what will be done to overcome any potential obstacles that may be apparent. This is the first part of a business plan that an investor will read. With this point in mind, identify within the Executive Summary the overview of the startup business and stay positive.

3. Mission Statement

What is the purpose of the startup business? A Mission Statement is, quite simply, a definition of what an organization is striving to achieve, how it is working to achieve objectives, and why it exists.   Too often, businesses overcomplicate a mission statement and get lost in the identity of what the business is attempting to portray to employees, customers, and the general community.

As an entrepreneur, you may have a million and one ideas rolling through your head and you probably want to incorporate each of the ideas in a mission statement. As you are well aware, this is not possible to achieve, and simplification is vital. To help combat this urge to put too much into a mission statement, first complete a valuable activity in writing down the primary ideas that you have floating through your mind. After putting thoughts to paper, go out into the World Wide Web and search for some of the businesses or organizations that inspire you as a leader and entrepreneur. On the same paper that you wrote ideas for mission statements for the startup, write down mission statements from some of the top organizations that you feel reflect positively in commerce. After comparing mission statements from organizations that you find inspiring, look for key words or phrases that stand out among them. Using a combination of what inspires you along with what your thoughts were for a mission statement previously, work to create a combined statement that will incorporate vision for the future as well as a foundation for what your business will work to achieve.

If you are getting a case of writer's block and are looking to find inspiration in developing an impactful mission statement, here are a few organizations to look into for inspiration:

- Patagonia
- American Express
- IKEA
- Nordstrom
- JetBlue

These businesses have been able to develop visionary mission statements that may assist in your business journey as well.

4. Company Objectives

Company objectives help to provide a foundation for what the business is going to achieve over a specific time period. Objectives for the business should be based on a strategic planning outlook for the future and should include an overview of distinguishing factors that will lead to the success outlined by the objectives. Company objectives identify where the business is going and provide the foundation for what actions will be described and broken-down further for the remainder of the business plan. Furthermore, company objectives will be continually used by employees and leaders of the startup to strive for the same overarching goals, even though responsibilities may be vastly separate depending on the business need[i]. A company objective helps potential investors and personnel to have direction and an expectation of how the business will essentially operate into the future.

5. Management Structure

When establishing a business or organization, one of the first items that need to be completed is identifying what the structure of the business is going to be. Structure in business has multiple levels, starting from a macro-level, identifying the entity type of business that is being established, to advisory structure, to management. When establishing management structure, as a part of a business plan, continue to think large with the ability to act locally. The following section will break down the start of every organization, the entity that will be the foundation for any action moving forward.

Business Entity Options

The structure of every business starts with the decision that must be made to adopt a business entity within the state that the business is operating, or multiple states if the organization will be performing sales and services in multiple locations across state lines. Entity options include Sole Proprietorship, Partnership, Limited Liability Company, Corporation, etc.

Sole Proprietorship

One of the most common forms of business structure to establish is a Sole Proprietorship, in that it is basically stating that an individual is operating as both a natural person and a business at the same time. However, even though a sole proprietorship is very easily established, there are potential downsides that can come into play, especially when looking to create buy-in from potential investors. In a Sole Proprietorship, all liability falls on the individual; this means that if the business is providing a service for a client such as repairing a roof and a ladder falls, injuring the client standing nearby, all of the liability for medical bills and damages will fall on the individual acting as the business. Additionally, this would mean that all personal assets would be liable for claims, so personal homes or property, or assets in a personal savings account could be held liable if a claim were to occur.

The tax situation is both simplified in some ways and complicated in others when it comes to a Sole Proprietorship. All taxes are filed under the individual's taxes, which make the logistics of filing simple, but the ability to track business expenses versus personal expenses is complicated.

So, the answer for you in this regard to developing a business plan is: stay away from a Sole Proprietorship, especially if the goal is to realize investors. Think big, act locally.

Partnership

A Partnership is similar to a Sole Proprietorship in that liability falls upon individuals, but in this case, the business would be developed by more than one individual. So if two individuals, let's say Sara and John, decide to start a hair boutique and begin conducting business, they have established a partnership. Taxes, similar to a Sole Proprietorship, are also filed under individual tax basis, unless what is known as a Limited Liability Partnership is established with a separate EIN for the business. Similar to the recommendation as Sole Proprietorship, stay away from a Partnership when looking to establish a startup, especially if the goal is to attain potential investors.

Limited Liability Company

Taking slightly a little more effort to file with the Secretary of State, a Limited Liability Company (LLC) entity is definitely worth any addition time spent creating. A Limited Liability Company does just what the name implies, it limits the liability of an individual that is in pursuit of performing business activities (You) and places the liability on the business itself. Taking our example from earlier, if a business is helping to repair a roof and a ladder falls on a client, injuring them, the extent of liability will only go as far as the assets held by the business, the individuals within the business are not held liable as long as there was not personal-negligence involved, such as drugs or alcohol.

There is an ability to file taxes either as an LLC, separate from an individual with a Tax Identification Number granted by the IRS, or the option to file taxes through a process known as Sole Owner Limited Liability Company, where taxes can also be filed under an individual's annual tax filing.

Corporation

Taking the step further in limiting liability and separation from an individual, a corporation designation requires a little more paperwork through a Secretary of State office and also requires separate filings for taxes. In addition to filing with the Secretary of State and IRS, Corporation issues common shares, providing voting rights to the organization at an annual Shareholders Meeting that would be held, and the shares themselves would be entitled to receive net assets of a corporation upon dissolutionii. A Corporation releases liability from the individuals and owners within the organization, similar to a Limited Liability Company, and also requires a board of advisors or board of directors to act as a governing body over the business being established.

From the standpoint of looking at a business plan and trying to decide between the various options of an entity to establish for the startup business, the two primary options will be to consider a Limited Liability Company or Corporation. Investors, more often than not, will most likely lean toward wanting the business to be established as a Corporation, with the thought of having actual ownership in the organization through share allocation.

Advisory Structure

Even though a Corporation is the only entity that is required to have an advisory board, it does not mean that any other form of business cannot have one. Surrounding yourself with local business leaders, entrepreneurs, and experts of fields such as business law is always a good idea. An advisory board is an integral piece of management structure, in that individuals that have varying perspectives and experience, can weigh in on recommendations on how to proceed from a strategic or visionary standpoint for the business, from a startup to veteran phase. An advisory board can be established with individuals that may be known from previous employment or companies associated with, trusted friends, industry experts, members of nonprofit organizations or additional boards, etc. When looking to find individuals to build an initial advisory board, it is optimal to attempt to find those that have walked in similar footsteps that can bring skill sets and experience to the table that will help the startup to succeed into the future.

Leadership Structure

Going beyond management, the business plan should incorporate the vision of leadership that will be expectation within the startup. What will you, as an entrepreneur, inspire through continual innovation techniques, leadership development in others, and building an environment of trust among additional team members that will be a part of the organization? These fundamentals of leadership, in an overview, should be included at this point in the business plan. Leadership goes beyond managing others, by helping to inspire through change that will occur at any level of organization through the continual business cycle. Identify leadership vision or actions that you will either help to develop in the hands-on leaders in the startup, or in your own development and actions if you are holding the integral role. Much of this will depend on the type and size of organization.

6. Products and Services

Before any customers are earned or marketing plans are developed, a product or service must be identified that the startup business will be providing to a given marketplace to achieve the objectives at hand. Product-oriented business structures will need different information presented within a business plan as compared to a service-oriented business structure. Many businesses will offer both products and services and each must be incorporated into the business plan in this section.

Products

A product is a good, or widget, that is created to be sold to a specific customer base. Products that are going to be developed by the startup need to be analyzed in this portion of the business plan to reflect such information as cost of production, packaging needs, diversification of product lines, anticipated sales price, and the reason as to what this specific product offers that is going to be viewed as a competitive advantage over similar products and competitors in the marketplace. In addition, if there are apparent trends in the current marketplace for similar items, the fluctuation in sales price or forward-thinking coupon options during these downturns will be essential.

Services

Services that are going to be performed have essentially less logistic allocation as compared to product creation and sales, but services are just as critical to be portrayed in a business plan. When explaining services that will be performed in the startup organization, ensure to include any licenses, certifications, or continual training that must be maintained in relation to the given services. The development of service pricing may also vary as compared to product-pricing-strategies, in that a service may be priced at a per hour basis or per service basis.

To be able to effectively develop an analysis for services or products that a business will be performing, attempt to think from a third-party perspective and form the question: "What would I want to know most about the products and services as a potential investor or shareholder to this business?"

7. Customer Analysis

Without customers, there is no business. Customers are what makes the business cycle move forward for any organization; whether a business has been established for over 100 years and has a multi-national presence, or if they are a startup business establishing a local presence for the first time, customers are needed to fulfill any business objective. While presenting and developing a business plan, the analysis of the potential customer market is the foundation for creating future success.

Target Market

The first step in analyzing the business' customer base is to identify what the target market will be for the startup. Identifying the individuals that will most likely be purchasing a product or service from the business is of utmost importance as factors such as marketing and promotion will coincide with the market segmentation. When identifying the target market of the startup business, one should identify the demographics, analyzing factors such as:

- Age- Is there a specific generation that will be highlighted in the target market? Is the product or service identifiable to a specific age range?
- Gender- Is the product or service utilized by a primary gender? What are the feelings that given

genders have toward the industry or products and services that will be sold by the business?

- Location- Are potential customers living within a given geographic area? Is this product or service going to be marketable across multiple regions or will variations in markets cause for drastic changes in communication and promotion?
- Etc.- Provide additional demographic information such as income levels or education levels of the identified target market that will be applicable to business objectives

Market Need

The target market has been identified and the business has a goal in mind for individuals to be of focus. Next in the business plan, an entrepreneur can now identify the market need for the given product or service looking to be established by the business. In this section of the business plan it is key to identify if there have been expressed interests within the target market for the product or service and in which ways this has been communicated to be measured. For example, have there been public recommendations or levels of feedback given to the Better Business Bureau or Google Reviews stating a need or want for the startup's potential output.

Market need can also be described in this section of the business plan by identifying if the target market is either growing, shrinking, or in a static-environment. The market trend can be supported in this section by combining market demand with public data, such as local population statistics. Is the housing market in the geographic region in a boom with school expansions making the headlines? This is critical information to be able to include for a potential investor looking at a business plan because it provides support to sustaining sales and performance over the long-term. If you can identify, not only a need or want for the product or service, but the potential for that need to grow exponentially in coordination with population increase within the target market, that will equate to a strong bottom line performance in the eye of a potential investor. In comparison, if the business plan is strictly being created for personal use, the ability to identify market trends will be helpful as objectives for the business continue to unfold into the future.

In this section of the business plan, it will be vital to include visual representations of the market needs and analysis. By visually demonstrating market trends and examples such as that with population increases, the key point of market potential at-a-glance will align with investor satisfaction. This can be completed with the incorporation of such visual aids as charts, graphs and tables.

8. Competitor and Industry Analysis

Just as it is critical to do a thorough analysis on your customer base and identify the needs and wants of those that you are going to be marketing towards, it is just as important to conduct a complete competitor and industry analysis. Knowing your competition is being able to know yourself and know your target market through a different perspective. Sometimes it is important to be able to reinvent the wheel and sometimes it is critical to be able to jump on the same wheel that someone has been rolling on for years, but to be able to decide on which option or route to take as a business owner, you must understand what others have done in making decisions and how the results of those decisions have played out to results.

SWOT Analysis

In every good business plan, there will be at least one common characteristic- SWOT analysis. A SWOT Analysis, (Strengths, Weaknesses, Opportunities, and Threats), is designed as a powerful strategic planning tool for all levels of organizations and will help you, as a business owner, to gain greater perspective on your business and the industry surrounding it. Taking the time to develop a SWOT Analysis comes in two parts: business (Micro/Local) and industry (Macro/Global).

First, as a small business owner, you want to develop a SWOT matrix for your own business, as a perspective from what you either already know or from what you have a relative amount of confidence in being true as your business begins (This may be challenging if you have not had any direct experience in the business that you are starting, but not impossible). If your business, up to this point, has not had any direct experience that can be measured by a SWOT Analysis, then replace the business mindset with completing a SWOT Analysis on yourself, as a leader. As a leader and entrepreneur, you set the foundation for your small business and will be the one to guide the small business to success; using this SWOT Analysis will also help you to become a better, more knowledgeable, leader for this business.

SWOT, again, stands for Strengths, Weaknesses, Opportunities and Threats. Take the time to identify each of these for your business and use the following questions as guidelines to assist you in getting the information down on paper, thinking on a micro-level for your organization:

> *Strengths- What are the things that your business identifies as benchmarks for success? If there was one thing that your business would do day in and day out and do it well, what would it be? What is the most valuable asset of your business and how does it leverage your goals? What is something*

that either you or your business has been recognized for consistently?

Weaknesses- What is the one thing that you would remove or change in your business today to make your life easier? What is something that gets in your way of achieving success? What is something that has been said to you as being an action or process that could be improved or made better as compared to a current standard?

Opportunities- What is the next best thing for your business? What additional markets or clients can your business serve that it is not currently serving or selling to? What is something that your competition has not yet thought of that could put you ahead of the curve? What are the items floating in-between strengths and weaknesses that could be leveraged to become a strength? What training or education is available for you to become a better leader? Are there processes currently available, or not available, which may make your organization more efficient?

Threats- What would cause drastic change to the way that you do business today? What, if taken

away from your business structure, would cause
potential for failure or drastic loss?

Just as with your business, or yourself as a leader, a SWOT
Analysis should also be conducted on an industry level.
Maintaining the same approach of Strengths, Weaknesses,
Opportunities, and Threats, now think on a macro-level
and put down on paper the SWOT for the industry that
your business is involved in.

Strengths- What are the things that this industry is
known for on a positive level? What are the things
that the news or industry-related materials are
stating as being standout performance metrics?
What are the items impacting positives on the
bottom lines of other similar businesses in the
industry? What keeps the consumers coming back
time and time again?

Weaknesses- What are consumers saying they
want to change? Why have other businesses failed
in this industry? What are the greatest costs for
other businesses in this industry? What is the news
or industry-related media saying should be changed
about the current industry?

Opportunities- What additional technology or achievements would make this industry become more efficient or profitable? What additional markets or consumer-base could this industry pursue to become more profitable?

Threats- What regulations or laws are in place that protect the way the industry is currently operating, or what regulations or laws could cause a drastic change in the way processes are completed in the industry? What other factors would cause a dramatic shift in demand for the product or service?

As a business owner, taking the time to develop a SWOT Analysis for both your business and industry allows you to become more knowledgeable in the environment around you. You immediately begin to structure thoughts on how you can leverage strengths to overcome weaknesses and use potential opportunities to avoid threats in the marketplace. This is natural- you are a business owner and entrepreneur- you have a mindset for opportunity and positivity, and now you have the chance to leverage that positivity and begin putting it into action. Similar to a personal budget where variable factors may cause changes over time, it is a good idea to come back to a SWOT

Analysis every so often (At least once per year) and ensure that key items have not changed since the last time it was developed. By using a SWOT analysis beyond the initial business plan, it will help you as a business owner to stay ahead of the competition and in line with trends in the industry. Again, always think and act big, even if you consider your business "small."

Competitor Performance and Reviews

Google is a powerful thing. Use online search tools such as Google or Yelp to obtain reviews from competitors in the industry that you are pursuing. Gather review information and look for similarities or trends, both positive and negative, from what is being communicated by others that have previously engaged with the organizations. This will help you to gain a better understanding of your competition and either what they are doing well or on which they are probably aiming to improve upon. Also, this helps to paint a better picture for what not to do as you enter into the same industry with your small business. If, as a small business owner you are looking to provide a certain type of cookie, but a competitor received a review that those cookies were not wanted in that specific part of town, you may probable want to reconsider the cookie menu.

In addition to online reviews, information obtained from the Better Business Bureau and local Chambers of Commerce will be valuable tools in being able to measure what feedback or ratings have been given to competitors. By gathering this information, you are able to identify a benchmark for quality and service that you are looking to achieve or surpass within your own small business to gain a competitive advantage over the competition. How will you ensure that your ratings are higher than a competitor? Where did they fail and what are you looking to avoid?

Market Share Capability

Combining together customer and industry analysis, the following section of a business plan helps to identify a given percentage of the market the business will be able to reach, and how the startup will be able to continue to grow and develop that share of the marketplace. The information obtained from the previous SWOT analysis as well as competitor performance, aligned with market potential, combines the ability to identify market reach. The level of effectiveness will be somewhat speculative at this point, but providing a realistic range for which the business is believed to obtain within the market helps to provide the capability of achieving a bottom line objective of profitability. This helps to create an accurate picture for potential investors as to what the outcome will be both for them, as well as for the startup business, itself.

As a business owner and entrepreneur, the fact will always remain that the goal is ever-present to obtain greater market share. In addition to identifying what the initial expected market share will be for the startup business, utilize this section to also identify actions and strategy to increase the percentage of market share for the future. Similar to above, use information gathered from the SWOT analysis, combining strategies identified from strengths and opportunities, and then focus on the capacity to leverage the potential of the activities to gain critical market share. The ability to acquire greater market share will, in turn, provide for stability and sustainability in a competitive environment and enhance the probability of maintaining profits for a greater spectrum.

9. Sales and Marketing Strategy

What impacts your bottom line and the bottom line of potential investors for your startup business? Sales.

Sales are fundamentally at the foundation of every business model. Whether you are selling a product or a service, the ability to sell through your business and as an advocate for your business will determine success. Let's take a look at it from the perspective of a results oriented formula:

Business Actions + Effectiveness = Sales

The Business Actions that are highlighted for a business include, but are not limited to, the fundamentals of developing a diversified marketing strategy. Marketing strategies incorporate five basic principles: Product, Place, Price, Promotion, and Profit[iii]. Previously, we discussed the overview and incorporation of products and services as a part of developing a business plan, but in this section we look further at demonstrating Promotion and the additional fundamentals of marketing.

Advertising and Promotion Highlights

When communicating marketing strategy as a part of a business plan, one wants to be able to identify the structure at which advertising and promotion will aid in achieving business objectives. It is critical at this point in a business plan to stay focused on quantitative measurements that can be attributed to advertising or promotion strategies, especially for a business plan being developed for potential investors. The reason for focusing on quantitative measurements with advertising and promotion is because potential investors need to see what the outcome of X amount of dollars invested in advertising will result in what profit.

In addition to identifying what resources will be allocated to promotion activities, the effectiveness must also be demonstrated in the business plan. Effectiveness in advertising and promotion can be communicated in a business plan by giving an overview of how the startup business will gain market share within the given market or region in which business will be conducted. Examples of advertising and promotion strategy breakdowns can be highlighted as follows:

- Social Media Strategy- Identify ways in which the business will utilize social media access such as Facebook, Twitter, Periscope, or LinkedIn to develop an online strategy connecting with current and potential customers and clients
- Additional Online Presence- In the modern era of business structure, trustworthy and professionally developed websites and online presence is just as important as having a certificate of good standing with the Secretary of State. An online presence helps perspective customers or clients to gain an understanding of what the business provides in the way of benefits, not only potentially to themselves, but also to the communities that they are involved. In this portion of the business plan, it is important to give an overview of how a website will be maintained, what the online presence will offer to those viewing, and what will be any incorporated fees involved.
- Public Relations- Along with online presence, the ability to develop relationships with local media is also beneficial when establishing a startup business. In this portion of the business plan, it is

important to identify what newspapers, news stations, magazines, or community organizations the startup business will build communications with in the beginning cycle of business, such as with creating a press release

- Print Advertising- Even though social media and online presence is of critical importance in the modern era of business development, print advertising and promotion still holds strong with business plans such as billboard advertising, newspaper print, or even direct-letter campaigns. Taking into account what works best with your level of business and the amount of resources you are willing to allocate to advertising, communicate through the business plan what you plan on using to promote and achieve the objectives of the startup business.

The activities that are planned as a part of advertising and promotion are related to the ability to track the results of such activities. In addition to portraying how market outreach will be completed, develop a strategy for how results of advertising and promotion will be tracked. For example, online tracking may be achieved with click-thru advertisement analysis, or public relations tracking may be achieved with analyzing follow up from community organizations or media outlets. Also, the additional effectiveness within activities of promotion and advertising can be emphasized in the section by going beyond a basic summary of social media sites or print strategies. Use this section within the business plan to relate effectiveness strategies such as developing grassroots marketing plans or additional snapshots of print advertising that will be developed in the initial business cycle.

Sales Personnel

Will the business require the addition of sales and support staff? Will the staff be part-time, full-time, or contract-based? What is the outlook for additional staffing needs based on sales performance (either positive or negative)?

These questions, and more, must be taken into account in this portion of the business plan. Whether the product or service of the business is going to be directly marketed by you as the business owner, or with the assistance of multiple sales personnel, the proof must be communicated. Identifying what the expectation is for sales personnel and the strategies that they will use to achieve results will be critical. For example, if service-oriented, a sales team member for the business may be expected to have an X amount of conversations per week with the expectation of a given result which will impact the profitability of the business if achieved.

In addition to the expectation to what sales personnel will provide to the business, this section also allows for the communication of how team members will align with business objectives through their personal actions.

Whether this be the expected dress or uniform, or the tone at which business is conducted, the vision through actions of employees can be communicated at this point.

Business today will most likely be much different a year from now, and even more so five years down the road. Use expected performance metrics to identify how the personnel needs may also change during the same time periods and what will be the expectation as growth or changes occur during this timeframe. Also, be sure to provide reasonable allotment for negative downturns in performance, answering the question of if employees will be minimized during these times or allocated in different ways during this time.

Sales Forecast

The activities and effectiveness involved within marketing strategies have the primary goal of achieving results. The results within a business can be easily recognized as sales. A sales forecast is an integral tool that helps to provide an outlook for potential investors, as well as yourself as an entrepreneur, when looking at the roadmap that the organization will be following. With the goal and expectation that activities and effectiveness of those activities will occur over a given timeframe, the results will be yielded in the form of sales. By combining data from anticipated market penetration as well as effectiveness expectation through activities, a given sales forecast can be illustrated over varying time periods.

As variabilities increase dramatically the further you look into the "crystal ball" of business performance, it becomes more challenging to present a potentially accurate forecast of what sales will be. In the importance of developing accurate and reliable information within a business plan, limit a sales forecast to one or two year's outward, limiting high variability in performance indicators. In addition to providing a limited time-frame for a sales forecast, also provide one or two additional what-if analysis- for example, provide a sales forecast based on anticipated results, provide an additional sales forecast with a 10 percent increase, and provide yet another sales forecast with a 10 percent decrease as compared to the potentially realistic expectation of what will occur. This will help provide a what-if spectrum for business leaders to watch as well as investors to observe to see if performance is achieving higher or lower than anticipated results for a given time period.

10. Operations and Logistics

Where will business be performed and what will be the level of logistics processes needed to keep the business moving smoothly? These questions will need to be answered in this section of the business plan being developed.

Operations

The location of a business operation is one of the first questions that a perspective customer or client will search for. There are decisions to be made when allocating resources for where a business will be physically located or operated from. With the availability of technology and support services, it is possible that a physical location will not be needed for the startup business, or at least from the beginning phases until greater capital is developed. The decision to either operate from a physical business location or out of a home location, or virtual, must be described in the business plan with supportive reasons as to how this action will either assist in reaching the target market identified or help to minimize cost structure. If multiple locations are needed, based on a regional standpoint or further, the additional allocation of resources must also be broken down into cost-benefit analysis that can be easily viewed from a potential investor standpoint looking at the business plan. In addition to cost-benefit analysis, include contingency strategies if there are cost implications or additional variables that may cause for the need to be utilized at a given point.

If a business location has not yet been identified, use this section to develop criteria that will be followed to identify a location in the future. Include the factors of where the business needs to be located in order to meet the needs of the marketplace as well as the physical needs for effective business services. A primary example for identifying a specifically needed location would be that of a startup restaurant that would essentially require a very specific location that could suit the standards and requirements for the restaurant industry.

Logistics

In the balance of supply and demand, the ability to manage the process of logistics becomes at the forefront. This section of the business plan works to identify items ranging from hours of service to suppliers or third-parties that will be needed to maintain business flow. Logistics is the flow of products or services from beginning to end in a business, including procurement, physical movement, storage, and additional factors[iv]. Suppliers and logistics-chains become heavily integrated and sometimes thoroughly complicated in a product-oriented business structure. The goal in this section of the business plan would be to simplify the breakdown of what suppliers will be needed and how the distribution of products and services will be completed over various markets. Remember that you are the expert of your business and that it can be very easy to over-complicate descriptions or processes in a business plan; however, potential investors want to know the basic outlay of how business will be done and what will be the outcome.

11.Business Capitalization

Investors are the first source of developing business capital. In this section of the business plan, take the time to demonstrate how additional capital will be raised and what the expectation is from a potential investor. Business capital can also be raised beyond investors with financing activities or personal fund allocation. Develop a business capitalization plan that illustrates the amount of capital that needs to be raised within a given time period and also include the basic expectations as to where the capital will be allocated within the organization, such as manufacturing equipment used to achieve production goals. Also, continue to look beyond the initial phase of business development, and consider in this section additional capitalization techniques a year or more out in business performance that will maintain adequate levels of capital.

12. Financial Plan

Everything that has been discussed previously in a business plan builds upon the financial plan of a startup organization. Financial plans identify the lifeblood of a business and recognize how funds will flow from sales, capital development, and investment assets to production and expenses. The management of finances in an effective or ineffective manner can either help to create positive or negative outcomes for the business. At the foundation of any activity or vision that a business holds, there will be a need for financial planning. This point of the business plan will require additional quantitative measures as compared to previous sections as finance is held at a critically important level to potential investors. If your personal experience in finance is not as diversified or confident as you would hope when developing this section, do not be afraid of seeking additional assistance from a finance expert or CPA. The additional items to be included in this section can include, but are not limited to, the following:

- Break-even Analysis
- Projected Cash Flows Statement
- Projected Balance Sheet
- Start-up Expense Allocation
- 3-year Profit-and-Loss Projection

13. Appendix Items and Additional Resources

At this point in a business plan, you have been able to develop a specialized document that provides a unique insight to the startup business you are building and have been able to develop a reason for potential investors to help support the vision. In addition to the highlights and sections listed above, there are several additional items that may be included to help round-out the most effective business plan possible. These items include, but are not limited to:

- Business and Personal Credit Reports
- Personal financial statements
- Related legal documents, business filings, or existing contracts
- Property or lease agreements
- Patent-pending material or photographs
- Personal resume
- Additional relevant documents that feel appropriate

Additional Resources

In addition to establishing a quality business plan, there are additional resources that will be useful along the way to developing a startup business. Take the time to complete further research on the following resources and how they can assist in helping your business achieve strategic objectives and success:

- Tax Information- Internal Revenue Service (www.irs.gov)
- Small Business Administration (www.sba.gov)
- National Federation of Independent Business (www.nfib.com)
- Small business resources and ideas for Entrepreneurs (www.inc.com)

- Department of Labor (www.dol.gov)
- Legal Information (www.nolo.com)

14. Conclusion

At this point in a business plan, you have been able to develop a specialized document that provides the ability to earn the trust and buy-in from potential investors. In addition, a business plan can be continually utilized by a business owner or advisory group into the future to ensure that core business fundamentals are followed in an ever-changing environment. Now it is up to you, as your own best advocate, to use the resources that have been provided and paint the picture of your startup organization. This will be the beginning of an incredible journey and the business plan that you are able to develop will help guide the way to success.

---

i

www.ingramcontent.com/pod-product-compliance
Lightning Source LLC
Chambersburg PA
CBHW071829200526
45169CB00018B/1276